CHAOS AND SILVER LININGS

–

A LIFE IN POETRY

BY:

COLLEEN MULRONEY

PRAISE FOR

CHAOS AND SILVER LININGS – A LIFE IN POETRY

<u>An important glimpse into living with mental illness</u>

A raw, emotional and very honest first-person perspective of living with a mental illness, with glimpses of hope and the will of the human spirit to triumph. Colleen opens her mind, heart and soul in this revealing, autobiographical journey.

BOOKS BY COLLEEN MULRONEY

WAVES OF CHANGE – A BOOK OF POEMS © 2014

MOMENTS OF TRANSITION – A 2ND BOOK OF POEMS © 2015

PERIODS OF SELF-REFLECTION – A 3RD BOOK OF POEMS © 2016

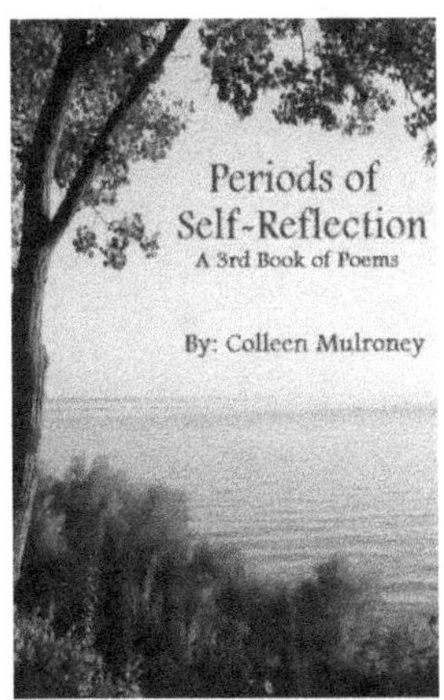

Chaos and Silver Linings

A Life in Poetry

Colleen Mulroney

DEDICATION

To each person that struggles with mental health...

To those who relate to the dark...

To the grim...

To the brighter days...

To the darkest days...

To those who relate and understand the struggles and the triumphs...

To those who walk alongside us...

To the friends...

To the families...

To the ones who see us and hear us...

To the ones who help us and support us...

To those who empathize...

Those who want to have a clearer picture...

Those who are trying their best to understand in their own ways...

To those who want to educate...

To those who want to raise awareness...

And to the many possibilities...

This book of poetry is for all of you!

Table of Contents

Table of Contents
THE IN-BETWEEN

Table of Contents

<u>THE DARK</u>

Table of Contents

Table of Contents

THE LIGHT

Encouragement for My Friends'

It's hard to find someone to trust.
Someone who is good.
Because I bet too often
You feel misunderstood.

It's difficult when you don't feel good in certain places.
Worried about the look on peoples faces.
Scarred and wishing you stayed in bed.
Cause you can't get the negative thoughts,
Out of your head

When you're feeling down
Don't try to fake it.
Just believe in yourself
And I know you'll make it.

It's hard when you feel all different kinds of pain.
But it's true to say,
This too shall pass.
Tomorrow is another day.

So, think about now.
Think about today.
Take it moment by moment.
And just believe,
That everything will be okay.

Self Love

I want to run free.
or spread my wings and fly.
I want to let myself be me.
Never give up and keep aiming high.

I want to live my life.
my own way
smile and dance.
Not caring what others say

Cause it`s not selfish to love yourself.
or put yourself first.
it`s not your ego talking.
When you write your own verse

it`s okay to feel sad at times.
it`s normal to feel emotions.
it`s how you deal with it.
And your attitude towards life's commotions

When I hear the saying
happiness is a choice.
I used to not believe it.
I'd listen to that negative voice.

But now I know it`s true.
cause I determine my own reactions.
to life's up and downs
I'm responsible for my own actions.

so, the points of this poem
is for you to hear your own voice.
take care of you, chose your attitude.
cause living your life is your own choice.

Hang On

Sometimes life gets too hard.
And you're not sure what to do.
And when you look at your deck of cards
and none seem right to play,
And you find your self thinking "not another day."

It's not time to give up the fight.
Somewhere out there
there is a light.
Don't give up when times get rough.
don't let go.
Hang on tight.

Sometimes we need to make a choice.
to let someone, hear our voice.
so, the feelings get out.
sometimes we may need to just shout.
and sometimes we may doubt.
that anyone can hear us
cause we may not be able to express ourselves.
in ways that others can understand
but look around you.
There may be someone holding out their hand.

Remember you're never alone.
even if you feel like that's what you've been shown.
and remember,
the sun will always rise in the morning,
and the moon gives light,
in the dark of night.
so, hang on to life.
don't hide from tomorrow.
in your pain and sorrow
don't let the bad times win.
your stronger than that
Hold up your chin.

I'm Not Broken

I used to think that my life was useless.
That I was here only to endure pain
I used to think that my life was worthless.
That I had nothing to offer and nothing to gain

I used to think that life was about hurt and doubt.
That everyone else was more important
I used to think that I was broken.
And that my life, my voice, and my visions didn't count.

But now I know that I'm not broken.
That I am strong, courageous, and amazing.
Now I know that I'm a good idea.
And that no matter what life may bring
I should have no fear.

Cause everything comes into our lives for a reason.
And for a long time that reason may be unknown
But until we learned that lesson
It will keep appearing in our lives.
Until we have understood it and grown

Now I know that I'm not broken.
That I am worthy of all good things
Now I know that I'm not broken.
I have my own song to sing.

Now I know that I'm not broken.
I am able to love myself.
Now I know that I'm not broken.
Because this is my truth
And these are the words to which my heart and soul.
Have made me a new and whole.

By the Water

Staring at the beauty of the world
Wrapped in its wonder and sight
I feel at ease, peaceful and free
Powerful in its possibilities and might

Surrounded by the colours of nature
I take it all in, deep breathes of pure fresh air
I inhale the memories and exhale the stresses of life
Forgetting hard times, feeling relaxed without a care

By the water my eyes observe the motion
as each wave ripples expand and grow
Each affecting the others destination and size
Each one reaping what they sow

A feeling of calmness overcomes me
And the hardest decisions seem like a breeze
for my mind thinks clearer
And my choices are made with ease

Hardships become a distant memory
Faded in to the background of my mind
Positive vibes take over
No negative emotions can I find

Relaxed now by the stillness of the water
Calmed by the gentleness of its flow
The quietness of my mind feels wonderful
As all the burdens, and stresses have been let go

My Own Beat

Walking down the street
I sing to my own beat.
no more worries, no more cares
Doing the things that before I wouldn't dare.

Life is great, life is good.
living the dreams of my childhood
feeling happy and free
isn`t this how life was meant to be.

Before life was stress and worries
caught up in the rush and the day-to-day hurries.
Trying hard to follow the rules of society.
being picky and choosy
about what to do, who to talk to and what to say.
I was living life like that everyday
but now who cares what they think.
They are going to judge you anyway.

So, let yourself feel peaceful and free.
Give yourself that liberty.
Live moment by moment
And cherish each second.

Don`t let others get you down or stand in your way.
this is your life, your one and only.
reach for the stars, reach for your dreams,
And never ever give up.

Life is what you make of it.
it`s not determined by the roll of dice.
it`s up to you, it`s always your choice
live for you, that`s my best advice.

© Colleen Mulroney

Coping

There is a light at the end of the tunnel
And no, it`s not a train
It`s about changing the thoughts
That are racing through your brain.

It`s about holding on to that little piece of hope
Finding different ways to cope
With all the stress, all the pain
Take it one moment at a time
Day by day
Go at your own pace,
don`t rush, life isn`t a race

Say what you need to say
Feel how you need to feel
Express it anyway you can
Just be safe
Use the safer ways to deal

Love yourself, it`s okay
Trust yourself; listen to what your heart says
Just take it moment by moment
And trust me
In the end it pays

Sometimes Things are hard to do

Sometimes things are hard to do
when life gets stressful
and difficult too
sometimes we need to do things we don't want to
And say things that are hard to say
but we must move on
Despite what may come our way

Life is full of good times and bad
happy times
and times that are sad
But we must continue down the road
Despite the heaviness of our load

Sometimes we must cry
Sometimes we need to say goodbye
But with every ending there is a beginning
So, they say
So, continue your journey
and I'll go on with mine
and at the end of the day
Look for the positive sign

Pen to Paper

Pen to paper is easy for me
but vocalizing how I feel
is so hard; I can't set it free.
So, I write everything down
to understand what I'm thinking.
whether I'm floating, swimming, or quickly sinking.

It's been my emotional release
since the age of thirteen
it has given me a chance at finding my peace.
cause holding everything inside,
eats away at my core.
tears me up and tries to kill me,
until I can't take it anymore

But today I'm becoming more self aware.
I know my defects, faults, and misperceptions
But I know how to change them, what to work on
I need to have faith, courage and find my strength
it must come from within, and all the positives around me,
because sometimes I purposefully choose not to see
all the good things in my life, and the people who let me be me.

but with change comes a fear, that scares me to the bones.
it brings tears to my eyes, and painful moans.
but not all change is bad, it could bring something more.
something even greater than I could possibly perceive.
I just need to have faith, open the next presented door.
and believe.

Spread Your Wings

I want to run free
or spread my wings and fly.
I want to let myself be me
never give up and keep aiming high.

I want to live my life,
my own way
smile and dance,
not caring what others say.

Cause it`s not selfish to love yourself,
or put yourself first.
it`s not your ego talking,
when you write your own verse.

it`s okay to feel sad at times.
it`s normal to feel emotions
it`s how you deal with it
and your attitude towards life's commotions

When I hear the saying
happiness is a choice.
I used to not believe it
I'd listen to that negative voice.

But now I know it`s true
cause I determine my own reactions,
to life's up and downs
I'm responsible for my own actions

so, the points of this poem
is for you to hear your own voice,
take care of you, chose your attitude,
cause living your life is your own choice.

© Colleen Mulroney

Work of Art

My life is a work of art
I will paint and draw, do what I need to do
I will fight each day to keep myself together
I will not fall apart; I will break through.

Life gives me obstacles, and challenges
but each wound can be covered with bandages.
each cut will heal and leave a scar,
but it's how I deal, and I'm a superstar.

I'm a fighter, and a warrior
I will get up each morning, face each day
it's my decision, my choices, my behavior,
that propel me through the darkest grey.

I will not give up, nor will I stand down
This is my life, I wear the crown
I won't give in, I have hope
I'm taking it moment by moment; this is how I will cope.

My story is not over yet, I have a lot to create
My life is a work of art
So is yours my friend
I hope you can relate...

© Colleen Mulroney

That Moment When

That moment when it's clear
that everything is going to be alright
when you know it in your heart,
that you're winning the fight.
When life's ups and downs,
don't hit extreme peaks.
when the storms and pain,
don't make you as weak.

When people's opinions
matter less than your own
because you know you're of value
you know you have grown.
When that day has come
were you can finally say.
I'm going to make it
moment by moment
through each and every day.

Courage

I am courageous
And I am free
I`m exactly who I want to be
I am healthy
I am beautiful
That`s what I see inside of me
It`s maybe not everyone else can see
But that`s okay with me today
Cause what`s important is that I know that I'm okay
There`s nothing anyone can say
That I'll let bring me down
Cause happiness is a choice
I don`t have to listen to that negative voice

Inside of my head
I have dreams
I have hope
And I believe in me
So, look out society
I`m not following your rules anymore
I`m living by my own
I`ve opened the door
To a world of opportunities
And endless possibilities
Because I`m not afraid anymore

A Stronger Woman

Today I'm a stronger woman
A woman peaceful and free
Because I know I'm worth it
I know I'm meant to be

I've been through tough times
Times that have been full of pain
But today I'm rising up
For I did not live those moments in vain

I have learned from my mistakes
And I know not what to do
So, I'm letting go of all the pain and sorrow
Looking forward to tomorrow

So, here's to each new day
To discover who I am
To dance and play with life
But I`ll never forget the pain and strife

Cause it made me who I am
How I see myself, and how I act
It made me a stronger woman
it just depends on how I react.

Don't Give Up

Sometimes things are tough
All uphill and really rough
Each day's a struggle
Just to get by
But keep on moving
keep aiming high.

Don't give up
No matter what you do
Keep on believing
And be true to you
Set small goals
Achieve them bit by bit
It's easier that way
When your hardest hit

Encouragement

Let out your feelings
Let out your fears
Let out all your emotions
And let out all your tears.

Scream, cry, yell or jump
Do anything you need to do
Don't bottle it up anymore
Cause its only hurting you.

Stop feeling so angry
Stop feeling so down
Start changing to smiles
No more sad frowns

Laugh, joke, have a good time
Care about yourself more
Go ahead spend that dime
Remember you're important
Many people care to
You need to start thinking
A lot more about you

Talking helps, but listen too
Many people want to help you
Change your attitude
Find who you are
Go on a hunt take your time
Just thank those around you
Who love and care too?

But realize yourself
How many people do care?
They support, encourage, yes, they dare
But only cause their spirits are kind.
And they know what it is
You need to find

© Colleen Mulroney

It's Your Life

You can always start over
When ever you desire
Close the book, Flip the page
Believe that you can always aim higher.

Trust yourself in everything you do
Follow your dreams, be true to you
Don't let others' opinions get in your way
listen to your heart, you have the final say.

No matter the trials you have faced
Continue to get back up, move at your own pace
Let the hard times make you stronger
Enjoy each moment, cherish the good memories a little longer.

Focus on your aptitudes and strengths
Challenge your weaknesses and you'll go great lengths
Believe in yourself, trust your abilities
Never stop dreaming about the possibilities

Cause your life is yours to live and to explore
Yours to do less or yours to do more
This is your life, own it every day
Remember this is your life, you have the final say

Just Hold On

Just hold on
think of those things that make you strong.
when times seem bad
and life's trials become too sad.
just remember the things that cheer you up.
remember the people that help to fill your cup.
Sometimes things can seem out of place
and it gets hard to run this race.
but never give up on life
cause all the pain and strife.
will go away.
someday

Keep Your Chin Up

Sometimes we focus on all our strife
And forget to look forward to everyday life
When things are rough
And life gets tough
Don't give up, keep your chin up

When your roses give you thorns
When the stars are hard to see
When it just gets hard to deal
And you're questioning what you feel.
Don't give up, keep your chin up

When everything seems rotten
Or maybe you're feeling forgotten
Try looking on the positive side
And find someone in which you can confide
Just never give up
And remember to keep your chin up

THE IN-BETWEEN

Stigma

Do you see the sad girl?
who cries almost every day?
or do you see the liar?
who says everything`s okay?

But you don`t know her.
yet you label and judge.
and when she gets mad
it`s you with the grudge
Do you see the sad boy?
getting picked on all the time.
Or can you see the man?
who never committed a crime?
But you don`t know him.
yet you label and judge.
and when he gets angry
it`s you with the grudge

stop and take a minute,
to think about the labels that you use
are they helpful or hurtful?
would you take that abuse?

cause you don`t know them.
yet you label and judge,
and when they get frustrated
it`s you with the grudge...

Waiting for the Moment

Feel like I'm going to crack
feel like I'm going to break tonight
the light in my eyes is fading,
but I got to keep strong, keep waiting.

I keep waiting for the change
the miracle within myself
for the moment when I care about me
my well being, my health.

Waiting for the moment in time
where I finally put myself first
not second, not last
because I'm not the ugliest, and I'm not the worst.
But it's so hard to believe
that I have value and worth
that I mean something to people
and have a purpose on this earth.

Because the thoughts inside my head
don't tell me the same things
they tear me down, try to break me
they've cut off my wings.
I'm falling, deeper than before
falling faster, can't hold on anymore
my strength and hope have vanished
I'm bruised deep into my core

but with one moment at a time
I refuse to give up
no matter how far I've fallen
I won't let myself letup.
Because it doesn't matter how many times, I've fallen
or how many times life's let me down
I'll just keep getting back up
because I refuse to be knocked down

© Colleen Mulroney

Afraid of Happiness

So afraid am I of happiness.
So scared am I of being content.
Each time I`m dealt a new hand to play.
I trick myself out of the light of day.

I focus on the negative
And everything going wrong.
I forget to live,
And sing my own song.

I hide in the dark corners of my mind.
I seem to feel safe there.
But then feel so left behind.
I forget myself; I forget who I am.

I sabotage my life.
And all things going well.
I run from the good
I prefer the pain.

For it`s something I know
To stay in the darkness and sorrow
But I want to see the light.
Feel the life and joy.

I think I deserve a rainbow.
After so much downpour, storms, and rain
I`m learning I have so much to offer.
So much to give and even to gain

I need to learn to let myself be free.
For there is only and will only ever be
One unique soul like mine
One individual like me

Would You Mind?

I don't know what to write today.
My mind keeps drawing blanks.
Should I write about happiness?
Or the reality of sadness and despair
Should I pretend to be happy?
Smiling without cares

Do you really mind if I express my deepest thoughts?
Despite how graphic or neurotic they may be
Is it ok if I share my life with you?
And everything inside of me,

Can I tell you who I truly am?
A person that was trapped inside herself.
who endured a life of horror and pain?
that came out of her bubble.
so not to live her life`s moments in vain

So, if it would make you feel better.
I decided not to keep all this to myself.
So, I can share my experiences with you,
and hope for the best.
It`s up to you
I`ll let you decide the rest.

Reaching Out

Deep black darkness
lost in the depths of despair.
can't find my own way out,
is anyone out there?

I'm reaching out for help, do you hear my cry
Don't leave me in this hole, I don't want to die
All the raw emotions and feelings
Have me craving the drink
to numb the pain and my thoughts
so, I can't feel and don't have to think.

Dealing with life sober
is an entirely different journey,
cause the road of drunkenness was leading my corpse to a gurney.
I was merely existing, waiting to die.
Today I want to live, watch the sun rise and set
knowing it will rise again tomorrow.
I've decided I don't want to drown in my sorrows

I've decided to reach out
and even though it's hard to speak, to vocalize my emotions.
I can take my pen to paper
cause the truth comes out as I write, there's no doubt.

so, hold my hand I'll need someone to walk with me.
sometimes my eyes may be closed shut, I'll need help to see.
sometimes I'll need a push, so I can feel free to be me.
sometimes I'll need someone to pop that bubble I hide within
please don't be shy, pop it with a pin,
for this is me reaching out
my voice can only whisper, but my pen can shout.

Here to Stay

Sometimes my life feels too tough to handle.
sometimes the wind keeps blowing out my candle.
sometimes I could use more will.
to keep me going up the hill

sometimes the levels of sorrows are high.
sometimes all I want to do is sigh.
sometimes life gets me down a bit.
but it's then I know I shouldn't quit.

even though I'm filled with doubt.
about whether I should tough it out.
I know it's now, I need to be stronger
to just keep holding on a little longer

Things have to get better one day.
time will pass and come what may.
through the good times and the bad
I've decided I'm here to stay.

Experience

My thoughts broke me.
Tore me apart and blinded me.
I was unable to see.
Who I was beginning to be,
A careless soul
Falling in a dark hole

My emotions numbed me.
Poisoned me and tortured me.
I felt nothing not even life.
Could only feel the pain and strife.

My eyes failed to see the light.
My body and mind lost the will to fight
I hit rock bottom and couldn`t look up
Wanting to stay grounded forever
Because I thought life could never
Never be happy, never be mine
That`d I`d never be able to grasp
The dreams I had in mind

I felt desperate and hopeless
Lost and alone
Even abandoned myself
Neglected and abused by my own hand
Like I jumped into a pit of sinking sand

But now I see the biggest obstacle
Is this demon, this monster in me.
To destroy myself when I just want to be,
Happy and free

So back to the fight, the everyday struggle
To live life and make it my own
But I am thankful for the experience
Because in this trial, this difficult moment
I cannot say I haven`t grown

Quiet Riot

I've got too much on my chest.
Feel like I'm not getting any rest.
The days seem long.
I'm trying really hard to be strong.
I feel like I'm doing so many things wrong.
I know I keep singing this same song.

But inside my soul there is so much pain
Trying so hard just to stay sane.
Some days I want to crawl out of myself.
Be anyone but me.
Some days I struggle.
Does anyone see…?

My emotions feel like they are having a riot.
But at the same time, I remain quiet.
Afraid to speak.
My voices just squeaks
But can you hear the words in my mind?
Screaming at me
While I smile and try to be kind
Someone come and set me free.

Some days it feels like there is darkness all around
Some days I feel like I'm going to drown.
Feels like there is so much distress and sorrow.
Maybe things will be better tomorrow.

Definitions

Adjectives, words, a poem
combining thoughts and feelings
into a stanza, or paragraph.
To describe the pain or joy
That not many can express.

Today I sit and write.
As I think about life, it's meaning.
My definition of life
The characterization of my life

What do I want to it mean?
How do I want others to remember it?
How do I live it?
Day by day, moment by moment
Negative emotions stir and spin around.
Like a tornado with no distinct destination
Wrecking havoc on my dreams, my goals, my hope
Leaving a path of destruction, self destruction?

Am I really defeating myself, self sabotage?
But how, I move forward, I dream big, I hope for a future.
But every time I get close, I run away in the opposite direction.
Fear...Fear of success, fear of being better or achieving more than my successors.
I can't do better than them; they would despise me, become resentful.
But aren't they already?

I know more than I reveal, think more than I say.
Hide more than I allow to be seen.
The pieces of me, parts of me that I can't describe.
No adjective in the dictionary can identify these fragments.
Some components I do not know, others I'm becoming familiar with
But there is no end...

This poem...has no end,
It is continual, never ending...
For it...it is my life.

The Reason

Why am I still here today?
For them can't you see?
The ones I care so much about
And steal my heart from me

They are the ones for whom I live
The reason that I breathe
Deeply in the air of life
They are the ones keeping me going
Pushing through all this strife

Without them I wouldn't be here
On this earth no more
No more worries
No more fears
No more red tears
Floating away from the shore
Gone forever I would be
Out of this crazy life
That'd be fine with me

Carefree (A poem from age 14)

Being carefree
Is how I long to be
No more worries No more fears
With a sense of peace always to take hold of me
I wait anxiously to be carefree Never have I felt that way
With every day comes a new fear
With every day comes a new worry
I can't wait for that day when I'm carefree
To be able to read a book without my mind drifting away
I dream of sleeping peacefully without waking up in a scare
Carefree how does it feel
To sleep through the morning and early to bed at night
To go to school during the day to go home in the afternoon
Carefree
A day with no cares seems impossible to me
Could it be, could there be a day
Where I can be carefree
My hands stretch out to take a hold of that day
But even my fingertips can't seem to reach it
Instead, I think of how my life could change
So, I could be carefree
But me, will it be, could it be,
That I be carefree
Troubles fill my days; fears control my heart
Sorrow hides my smile and cares fill my mind
Will there ever be a day
Where all my troubles go away
Where all my fears and all my problems are solved?
I pray for such a day
When only good things fill my mind
I long for the day when anxiety will let go of me
Today being carefree seems impossible to me
Tomorrow's the same
Worries and fears flood over me
So how could it be, will it ever be?
Oh, how I dream of that day
When I'll be carefree

Socializing

Socializing
Not something we do often enough
Get to caught up in our pain, lost in the rough
Tangled in a maze of broken pieces and stuff

Caught on the sharp edges, linked to it all by handcuffs
So stuck in our ways, we isolate, automatically keep people far away
But the longer they stay away,
our railway to decay adds tracks,
and it subtracts from our value and worth,
leaving us even more alone, lost,
until it becomes clear that we are the ones in a prison cell,
Put in a self-made hell, a jail cell,
Spinning around like an out-of-control carousel.

And still it takes a bombshell to dispel the lies we've told ourselves,
to say farewell, to rebel, turn off our auto drive and shift it to manual.
Then when we finally open the shades, let the light in,
it's so bright it's like being hit with lightning, a shock to the system.

Life

Life can be hard
When you feel stressed
And there's a lot on your mind
When you start to feel depressed

When you're not sure what to do
And there's no one you can find
To really talk to
And you start to feel all alone
And you want to cry
Just let the tears flow
And then you sigh

And you can feel that times are about to start
Getting harder and harder
And you smiles get father and father
Apart
But keep on going
Keep on knowing
That things will get better soon.
Cause even in the dark of night
There's a light
It's the moon

Setting Myself Free

Sometimes I don't know what I'm writing
I'm writing just to be
To vent all my feelings
And set myself free

When everything is building up inside of me
And I have no way to get it out
Poetry becomes my emotional release
A simple way for the pain to decrease

Sort of like a lifeline
A personal escape
When I don't want to burden others with my tears
Or scare them with my fears
Or with the things that have happened to me
Throughout the years

When I don't feel like talking
Or to worried to say a word
When too much is on my mind
But I want to be kind
When too much is bottled up inside
And the emotions I can't hide
And pain is too much to take
And a smile I can't fake

But sometimes I don't know what I'm writing
I'm writing just to be
To vent everything inside
And set myself free

My Walls

I've built up these walls
They stand ten feet tall
Reinforced throughout the years
They keep in my fears
They keep in my internal tears
But they keep others out too
Maybe they're keeping out you

I'm hiding behind them
To afraid to break them down
I'm used to hiding in this place
So, I don't have to show my face
Cause usually I'm a disgrace.

I'm fearful of what you might find
When you break down these walls
Or find a way to look behind
Please be kind
And keep in mind
That these walls we're built for life
Thought they'd keep out the new pain and strife

But they are blocking me from being me
Stopping me from being free
So, brick by brick
I'll take them down
So, you can eventually see
The real me

What Do They See?

People on the bus
Are staring at me
I can't help but wonder
What do they see?

Do they see my arms?
so full of scars
Can they see my soul?
Behind my self-made bars
Do they see the sad girl?
Who cries almost every day?
Or do they see the liar
Who says everything's okay
Now I close my eyes
And run away
Escape from reality
It's the only way
to get through some moments
to get through each day

I Try So Hard

Dying
Yet, Hanging on
These days pass by
From dusk to dawn

My thoughts
Consume me
Break me down
Scars speak to me
Without a sound
Remind me of a past
I thought I left behind
But there it is
Inside my mind

Hidden away
Only I can find
Truth, hurt
And memories
Real as blood
Flowing from my veins
I try so hard
To escape the pain
But

My thoughts
Consume me
Break me down
Scars speak to me
Without a sound
Remind me of a past
I thought I left behind
But there it is again
Inside my mind

At the Bottom Again

I've been giving up on myself
letting the dark thoughts in my mind
Letting toxic emotions take over
I've let myself fall behind

I've been crying, and hurting
seems all I can feel is the pain again
Been dying inside, numbness has taken over
I want it all to end, but will it and if so when?

But I don't want to end my life
I'm hoping it's just the storm before the calm
Having faith that this moment will pass
Just as fast as life dropped the bomb

But the bomb has fallen
And it's blown away all my hopes and dreams
So now I'm broken but holding on
Dealing with my silent and internal screams

Cause I want to, but I don't want to let go
of this life that seems full of only misery and pain
I feel stuck, trapped in a life where I feel no joy
Why am I down here, at the bottom again?

I Decide My Story

There are many things I hide behind my eyes
the pain, the sorrow, the tormenting thoughts
All hidden deep inside, where most can't look behind
Including the self-destructive thoughts of suicide

This hush, shush, taboo subject, that no one talks about
passing thoughts that are present in my everyday life,
Sometimes even the plans on ending my own personal strife
Leaves me alone, scared, and holding a knife

The darkness that consumes me, overrides my will
The weight on my shoulders as I try to climb uphill
The memories of my past, and worries about the future
Stuck in the middle of nowhere, held down by an anchor
And then the thought of actual death
The nothingness makes me ambivalent
The joy in taking one last breath

Yet the sadness of the permanent
Is this what I truly want, to end all forever
Or do I remind myself that everything is temporary
Do I become my own destructor, my own attacker?

Or do I remind myself that this is my decision, my story
I have the power to chose, if my story ends here
I also have the choice to reach out, despite my fear
I have the final say, if this is my goodbye
but I'll probably stick it out a little longer and look up at the sky.

Memories I Wish I Never Had

taking up space inside my head
memories I wish I never had...
they keep coming back to haunt me,
playing over and over in my mind

Torturing my soul, driving me crazy
Making everything I did all blurry and hazy.
They were just like a tenant destroying my space
so, I kicked them out, I just hit erase.

to my memories, you can`t drive anymore.
this is my soul, my personal core,
you had me down on my knees,
but look at me now, I`ve got keys,

This is my life; I decide where to go
I'm showing you I`m not scared to drive
I`m making my choice, hear my voice
it`s happening now, this is live

Bad memories ruined everything I built,
knocked them down with a single blow,
and I carrying around the guilt,
realized I have more to offer, and more to show.

Not going to be scared, no holding back
not even going to crack
so now that they`re gone, it`s time to renovate my place
and make it my own personal space.
Cause I'm breaking free
of these memories I wish I never had
just letting them go,
Letting myself grow
no more fears, no more tears
living for me, carefree,
doing what I want
I`m breaking free

© Colleen Mulroney

My Rules

Don't make waves
And avoid conflict
That's how I behave
I don't speak how I really feel
I tend to avoid what's real
So, I don't have to deal
These are the rules I live by
Even though they make me sigh
And sometimes I even cry
When I'm by myself
Alone
It's just how I've grown
But they don't do me any good
Even though at first, I thought they would
I've been through too much in my life
Been through too much pain and strife
But now I'm tired of living this life
I need to change my ways
In order to have better days
I need to speak my mind
Say what I need to say
No matter what the circumstances
No matter what comes my way

Standing Strong

I will not fall
I will stand tall
Despite what may come my way
Even though each day
It gets tougher
Harder and rougher
But I'm going to make it
Take it bit by bit
One moment at a time
Even if we are without a dime
And the stress
Is making me feel like a mess
Even if my body is aching
And I can't get any rest
But I will do my best
Cause I will not fall
I will continue to stand tall

© Colleen Mulroney

It's OK

Don't give up, I won't give up
I'm going to keep fighting,
Each day, each moment
But I'm tired, so tired.
Fears, insecurities, are surrounded by need.
The need to be loved, heard, and free.
But what is free? Free from me?
Or free from societies standards
Or free from my deep core beliefs that I'm no good.
How about instead of free, I say acceptance?
Acceptance of self ... acceptance of others
Despite the fright of not being accepted,
Or of being secretly hated, or ridiculed,
But what if I said need or desire
Because I have the need to feel appreciated
The need to feel valued.
But now what if I said?
That everything comes from within first,
A scary thought, from someone who's terrified,
Terrified of loving herself, of accepting herself.
Because all the way down to my gut I feel that it's wrong
That deep down, I feel like a bad child who deserves to be punished.
But what if? What if I tried or fight...?
A concept that lingers in shallows of my mind,
Somewhere deep in the hidden valleys of my thoughts,
I wonder what if I loved myself first.
I wonder what if I accepted myself first.
What if I believed in myself first?
A thought, a thought that these wonders deserve more attention.
So, because I also hear: "don't give up."
I won't give up.
I will fight for the right to love myself.
I will fight for my right to be a person that accepts me.
I will fight for my right to be,
Because I am who I am,
I am me! And that is okay!

© Colleen Mulroney

Stuck in My Old Ways

Trapped behind self made bars
Steel bars built of perception
Stuck in my old ways
and my own deception

I put myself down
until I'm five feet under
almost buried in my own dirt
and all I can do is wonder.

How I got this low
but deep inside I know.
My thoughts, my points of view
How I treat myself, what I do

it all adds up bit by bit.
How I feel about myself
a worthless piece of shit
How I treat myself

isn't' how I treat everyone else,
they are silver and gold.
I collect dust up on the shelf
I blame me for everything.
even when it's not my fault.
I take everyone's responsibility
but these ways need to come to a halt.

I need to let myself be happy
and take the actions to achieve whatever that may be.
I need to sing my own song and dance my own dance
I need to hold on and give myself a chance

Will I?

Will I ever find?
That person who cares
Will I ever find?
A person who will always be there
Will I ever find?
That person who can help me
Will I ever find?
That person I'll trust with all my heart and soul
Will I ever find?
The person who will take me away
Will I ever find?
A place of peace
Will I ever find?
The place where I can be happy
Will I ever find?
The place where no conflict is about
Will I ever find?
The place where love and happiness explode
Will I ever find?
The place where I'm accepted
Will I ever find?
The place where help can be found
Will I ever find?
The place where illegal things don't take place
Will I ever find?
The place where there's no abuse
Will I ever be?
Happy, with a real smile upon my face
Will I ever feel?
Peace and comfort on the inside
Will there ever be a day
Where I can say I love my life and myself

Time for Change

I took a long hard look at my life
and realized I'm tired of all the strife,
it's causing to much pain.
I've now got too much to gain,
When you're in the darkness
and you can't see the light,
perhaps it's time,
to put up more of a fight

It's time to fight for my life
Now one day I want to be a wife
cause I've come a long way,
and I've made a lot of mistakes,
but now it's a new day,
I'm walking a new path
creating my own way
And I'm making changes that are going to stay

Sometimes I might be feeling a little run down
and some days it's harder not to frown,
But I can beat it
I've been harder hit
and I'm still breathing,
even feeling

Now I'm tired of your taking
and I'm tired of the faking.
I've found a new strength can you see
It's a better part of me
I've never felt this good
always been sunk so low,
but now take a look at me
cause I've got something to show.
I've come a long, long way
Seen the skies at their darkest grey
but now I'm choosing life,
now I'm here to stay.

© Colleen Mulroney

Internal Pain

I'm trapped
Inside myself
All alone
Suffocating
From my life
Cornered in darkness
Under stars
Crimson tears
Falling down
I'm drowning
In my sorrows
Bleeding
From my wounds
Dying slowly
From the scars
Hidden inside

With Time

Going through tough times
Always makes you stronger
We always want to get through it right away
But it usually takes a little longer

I`m hanging in there
I`m holding on
Listening to my music
Singing the lyrics to the song

Writing in my journal
Words to set things free
Words to get the pain out of me

It`s time to love my body
Time to get back on track
To give myself a pat on the back
Because I've been here before
Just never this low
But moment by moment
I get better with time
This is what I know

My Eyes

It's the twinkle in my eyes
that give it away.
if it is faded or bright
it depends on the day.

it is my personal storyteller.
of whether I am okay
my not-so-secret keeper of thoughts
when I do not have any words to say
It's the gate to my soul
your inside look
some can read my emotions.
like reading a book
Everything is known through my eyes
Everything is said without speaking a word.
Everything is felt without shedding a tear
even my happiness and even my fear

A Scary Thing

Happiness
is a scary thing.
when all you know is pain
hurt caused by others.
or pain inflicted on yourself.
when you can't see the light
or what your life has to gain

happiness
is a scary thing.
when you've never been happy before
when you've never looked beyond your door
when you're used to sadness,
and painful emotions
when you haven't felt well enough
to simply want more
Happiness
is a scary thing.
when you don't know its name
or its feeling, just the same
when you're used to losing the game

Happiness
is a scary thing.
but I'm going to face it.
take it step by step.
and sometimes I may want to run and hide.
or need to be by someone's side.
but I'm not going to run away.
Because I want happiness
to be here to stay

© Colleen Mulroney

THE

DARK

Chaos

I'm a jumbled mix of ups and downs.
a whirlwind of emotions
racing thoughts going so fast.
Each one causing a personal commotion.

I am a bleeding wreck of a person.
that believes to have only one way out.
I'm swallowed in my own tornado.
Where no one can hear my shouts.

Deeply ambivalent about life
The to be or not to be question.
tired and confused by all the strife.
yet fighting and holding on with aggression

Screaming chaos in my mind
falling down and sinking
running out of breath to swim
Someone help stop this thinking.

All alone and scared of the darkness.
the monsters I hear and see in my head.
unable to function and pretend I'm okay.
all I can do is stay hidden in my bed.

Alone

I feel so lonely.
So helpless, so hopeless
I'm so scarred.
I'm falling into despair.
But I don't care.

My heartaches with sadness
I feel alone in the world.
No one to talk to
Nothing to do.
I feel so upset.
I want to cry.
Black is all I see through my eyes.

This is not the way I want to feel.
But I can't climb out.
And there's no door.
I need some help.
But I don't know where to go.
I sit alone for hours.
With nothing to do

So, my mind is open,
To haunt me with ugly memories
My smile is lost under the ashes,
Of the burnt-out flame of my soul
My happiness and joy are locked up,
But I have no key.

I might laugh around you,
And smile and joke
But inside I feel like I'm about to choke.
I know I really need someone to talk to
But I'm so in despair.
Now I really just couldn't care.

© Colleen Mulroney

Laying Down My Sword

Bricks are being thrown at my head
Damn it I'd rather stay in bed
Life is getting too hard
I want to be dealt a better card

But hope is a fantasy
Not a reality
Struggling just to stay alive
Trying hard to survive

Each day that passes
Are filled with dark clouds
The visions in my head
Are getting so loud

Depression wants to win really bad.
All the time I feel like crying
I feel so sad
So tired all the time
Trying to fight
I want to lay down my sword
Let them kill me
And give in to the light

Life is beating me black and blue
I don't know what to do
Trying to stay positive
Trying to believe
But I just need some relief

© Colleen Mulroney

Falling Fast

Darkness is surrounding me
It shadows my soul
It's taken me hostage
It has taken control

I used to feel
something inside of me
That would glow in the dark of night
It would fight away my demons
It would take away my fright

Keep me focused and strong
Keep me breathing and alive
Even when things were going wrong
But now I feel so lost and alone
I'm missing that something in me
That was making me happy
That was setting me free

I feel so sad, like giving up
I've been like this in the past
But I'm falling again
just never this fast

Anxiety

My chest feels tight
My mind filled with fright
Nothing's alright
I'm trying to put up a fight
But my eyes are closed tight
So, I can't see the light

I'm falling
I'm screaming
Without a sound
I'm down
On the ground

Can't fall anymore
My mind aches
And my body is sore
Panic overcomes me
I can't take anymore

Someone come help me
Please set me free
Get rid of this feeling
Anxiety let me be

Shaking Inside and Out

Shaking inside and out
Feeling so much doubt
Too much inside me
Got to set it free
Feeling overload
Good and bad
Feeling okay
But at the same time
Simply sad
These feelings are overwhelming
So many things that I must face
I don't want life to fall out of place
Trying so hard
To keep up my pace
Don't want to fall again
Fallen to many times
Got to stay on my feet
Personal expectations to meet

Some things I've got to change
Or I'll follow the cycle
But it feels strange
And every step is hard
Difficult to talk about
The cards
I've been dealt
It's like there's a belt
Tightening around my neck
when I try to speak
And sometimes after
I'm a wreck
But it's good to get it out of me
Been bottled up for so long
To hard to always be strong
Sometimes you got to cry
Scream and let the tears out
But then I'm shaking
Inside and out

© Colleen Mulroney

Alone 2

Sitting inside my room
the walls close in on me
My thoughts take control
Someone set me free
I heard a voice
But I'm all alone
I don`t know what it said
It was more of a moan

I`m surrounded by friends
yet feeling all alone
uneasy and nervous
Wishing I was home

Did you see that?
sometimes what I see
isn`t there at all
making me freeze
and my body just stalls
What are they thinking?
Why do they stare?
What are they thinking?
Why do I care?
I`m surrounded by strangers
yet feeling all alone
uneasy and nervous
Wishing I was home
They`re laughing at me
pointing and staring
taunting me and teasing
instead of caring

Now I'm surrounded by family
yet feeling all alone
uneasy and nervous
Wishing I wasn't home

© Colleen Mulroney

Yesterdays

Memories of bruises and tears rolling down my cheeks,
the screaming and yelling still echo in my ears.
the present everyday reminders of their critiques
because the pain of yesterday has lasted for years

Was I never good enough, was I never lovable
was I always in the way, or a piece of trash, was I disposable?
Will I ever feel worth it, Will I ever love myself?
Will I ever take myself down from collecting dust upon the shelf?

Will I ever feel worthwhile of living my own life?
being happy, enjoying the moments, doing things for me
Will I ever feel serenity, at ease and peaceful
Will I ever be able to forget the hurt, and be set free?

Because the little girl inside of me is crying
screaming out for love and attention
but now on the outside I am an adult.
I feel the need to hold the pain in and sit in detention.

But why should I be trapped, behind self made bars
why should I let my past define who I become?
is every day not a choice, another chance to breathe in fresh air?
to do something different, simple because I care

It's hard to care about myself, when as a child the validation wasn't there
but today it must come from within, a personal decision to love who I am.
who I want to become, following my dreams and listening to my heart,
because deep inside I know this is the beginning, my new start.

Nightmares

How do you deal
How are you supposed to feel?
When you want to scream
Because you're afraid of your dreams

When they make you feel all alone
When they remind you of a past all too real
When all you want to do is groan and moan
When the time comes to sleep
It's a fear that runs all too deep

Afraid to close your eyes
Afraid of what you'll see
You wonder why
Why won't they let you be?

One is too Many...

One is too many, and bottles not enough
I crave that first drink, that sets off the rest,
to escape my mind, to run away from the pain,
to ignore the fact that I'm depressed.

But one will be too many, and bottles never enough
to numb the emotions and feelings inside of me.
instead, it will cause more problems, and trigger the train,
a commotion of disasters, and my own boat will be lost at sea.

Lost in an ocean at which my boat could sink,
and I could surely die,
so why take that first drink
why believe the lie.

The lies that repeat in my head
that one drink could solve my pain,
take me away to a better place,
this is the disease inside my brain.

It's cunning, baffling, and powerful,
just waiting for me to let my guard down,
waiting for me to question myself, and my faith,
waiting for me, doesn't say a word, doesn't make a sound.

But with help from others, faith, and a program
that rescues me from myself.
I have a chance at life, and recovery is possible
my mind will get better, so will my health.

It's called believing and trusting something greater than me
it's called faith, hope, love, peace, and forgiveness,
it's a place where I can be free,
A place where I have the freedom to be me.

A place where I in fact don't need the drink,
and have tools in place to fight the battles in my head,
in which before I would have let myself go
but now I listen, pray, and have faith and hope instead.

© Colleen Mulroney

THE
DARKEST

Content Trigger Warning
(Suicide, Self-harm)

Reason to Be

When will my time come...do you ever wish you could fast forward life,
to quickly get a glance of the future to know if all the pain, the suffering,
the keep going attitude will be worth it, not be in vain.

Because when the days become mountain's and cliff's, it's utterly exhausting.
Ups and downs, round, and rounds.
And time becomes something you constantly countdown,
and sound becomes music to quit the background, that has turned into a never-
ending battleground.

No one knows every part of me,
not even myself...to many missing pieces.
And the more I'd tell you,
the chances increase that your company and understanding or empathy will decease.

I feel like I'm all alone, I can't help it you accidentally see some of my scars,
the tip of the iceberg that goes as deep as the seas rock bottom.
My past and mind is so dark that the sea freezes.
My mind is full of things that could cause diseases,
and the only thing my ability allows me is to be clear on is I'm my own detainee.
My eyes are closing weighted by the effects of medication.

Running on Empty

I'm fed up with being here
So beaten and scared
Tired of the pain
This life's too hard

I'm running on empty
Crawling on the ground
The weight of my past
Pushing me down

© Colleen Mulroney

Silent Storms

Withdrawn, quiet, lost in the flow of toxic thoughts.
Waves of emotions flooding my lungs... I'm drowning.
Darkness, hopelessness, there's no air.
Silently screaming through crimson smiles,
quickly suffocating underneath the weight of my despair.

I'm not meant for this world, for this life.
I hold the control but no power over its side effects.
The hurricane of devastation that would rip through the souls I've touched.
I couldn't offer consolation towards the pain all because I wanted mine to end so
much.

Have You Ever?

Have you ever...
Walked across an overpass.
Looked down and wanted to jump?
Have you ever...
Walked along the waterfront.
And wondered if it could sweep you away?
Have you ever...
Held a piece of rope.
And wondered if it could support your dead weight?
Have you ever...
Held a knife.
And wondered if it was sharp enough to slice through veins?
Have you ever...
Observed a gun.
And wondered how quick the bullet could end your life?
Have you ever...
Thought about electricity.
and wondered how many volts it takes to stop your heart?
Have you ever...
Crossed the street without looking.
Hoping a large vehicle would hit you?
Have you ever...
Been inside a metro station.
And wondered when to jump?
Have you ever...
Stood on a set of train tracks.
And wondered if you should move?
Have you ever...
Held a bottle of pills.
And wondered how many it would take?
Have you ever...
Thought about suicide.
And the many ways in which you could end your life.

Silence

Sitting Inside This Room
The Walls Close in On Me
My Thoughts Take Control
Someone Set Me Free

Trapped Inside This Body
Hiding in My Mind
Sitting In A Dark Corner
That Only I Can Find

Crying Through My Wounds
Red Tears Falling Down
Crying Like A Fountain
But I Don't Make A Sound

Suffering In Silence
Not Visible To The Eye
The Only Words Out Of My Mouth
Are Deep Long Sighs

A Cutters' Moment

Sitting in the darkness
Pins push through my skin
The chill of pain
Spreads through my body
The fear, the panic,
My head starts to spin

Racing with thoughts
And memories
Moving ever so slowly,
Getting faster n' faster
Faster until I can't breathe

Pain seeks me, I need it
Like a drug, with out it I suffer
It loves me, and I love it
The feeling of tearing, bleeding flesh
Is cooling, and relaxing

Everything pauses, nothing else matters
Only the need, the burning desire
For my blade, for my pain, for my blood
A painless, tearless release
The flow of crimson red tears
Through my pale thin skin

Numbness passes through my body
And through my mind
I'm emotionless, I feel nothing
Can't think, can't stop, can't feel
Finally, I win

A flick of the knife, a little pressure,
The flow of blood, the heat
Escape away from reality
I let the past fall behind

© Colleen Mulroney

Stuck

Thoughts of suicide
Spin me round and round
Cutting keeps me safe
Away from underground

Thoughts of suicide
Filling the dark corners of my mind
Cutting is the better option
The only I can find

Hurting so much on the inside
Cutting sets me free
To many thoughts of suicide
Let me cut, let me be

Somewhere I'm trapped
Trapped inside of me
Stuck with thoughts of suicide
Please cutting set me free

Lost in a world of darkness
Pain surfaces on the outside
Bleeding wounds that help me cry
Perhaps it's better if I die

Dark Clouds

Dark clouds looming over me
Blurring my vision
Making it hard to see
All I can see is black and blue
Just like the wounds on m soul
Covered in tears and scars
From falling in deep dark holes

Now I've fallen, and fallen hard
I'm tired of getting up
I don't see the point anymore
Why continue to fight
There's nothing left in my cup

Why fight for something that's not worth it
I'm not worth it; I'm a piece of trash
That gets used when needed
Then forgotten, no wonder I crash

I want all this to end
I'm so tired, no more
I'm saying in m dark corner
And locking the door

I'm tired of getting hurt
I'm tired of getting burned
You'd think from experience I'd have learned
I'm tired of all the pain
There is nothing left to gain

People are better off without me I mean
These are the thoughts in my head
This is the way it seems
So I've decided I'd rather be that statistic, something that has value
It's the least I can leave the world with
My last effort, something I can do

Shutting Down

I'm tired of talking
I'm tired of the pain
I'm a burden to others
All I do is complain

I'm tired of trying to cope
Tired of fighting to believe
In the fading hope
I feel I've reached a point of no return
I'm caught in the fire
And I'm ready to burn

Cause I'm tired of the thinking
I'm tired of reality
Of trying to be a part of today's society
I'm tired of my thoughts
I'm tired of my mind
I'm tired of looking
For things I can't find

I'm tired of trying to believe
In the hopes of tomorrow
But with each day that passes
I'm filled with more dread and sorrow

So now I'm going away
To a place inside of me
Cause I don't care anymore
What happens to me
I need to be numb
I'm so tired of the fight
I can't even sleep peaceful dreams at night
My dreams are filled with terror and fear
I really don't want to be here

© Colleen Mulroney

My Escape

What do you want me to say?
I can't just snap my fingers
And make it all go away
It's an addiction they say

It was an escape
I thought I could control
But cuts turned to gashes
Minutes to ashes
And blackened my soul

Desire

Desire
Want, need, dying need
Such an addiction, so powerful
Besides my thoughts, the scars
My scars chant, more they want more
They haunt me
Reminding me of the pain
Reminding me of the feel, the release
The beautiful flow of crimson red tears
Flows, bleeding down my white skin
Deeper, deeper, how far can you go?
Can't feel anything anymore
Sometimes I get so numb
Can't feel anything
No pain, no gain
Pain feels so good

Hopeless

What do you want to do with me?
Lock me up, throw away the key
I don't care anymore, I'm already dead
Everything's to messed up inside my head

I'm feeling so lost, so far away
And nothings going to bring me home
Nothing you can do, there's nothing to say
I'm stuck in this darkness all alone

My tears aren't clear, They're bloody red.
Flowing from the gashes in my flesh
I don't want to move, or get out of bed
No, its nothing you said
It's this feeling inside of me
The thoughts in my head
I'm longing for peace
Longing to be dead

In the Darkness

Thoughts are taking control
Of her body, mind and soul
Dragging the blade deep
Watching her blood seep

Hiding behind her wall
Reinforced, so it won't fall
Thickened by scars
No one can get through her bars

Lying behind her beaten skin
Preferring to be all alone
No one can hear
Her years and suffering moans

In the darkness she hides
Left to dream about suicide
No one is supposed to know
About her pain and crimson flow.

Now I Know

Shaking in my bed at night I cry
The want, the need, the urge
Ways to destroy my body
Inside and out
Some visible to the eye
Others not....
My body is craving them
My mind is screaming just one more time
But my soul is weak and hurting
I don't use these ways to enjoy life
But to forget it, to avoid it, to runaway
From my feelings...
From my emotions...
From my thoughts...
To do anything in my power, or so I thought
To pretend that my life wasn't happening to me
That my life was a dream, a nightmare
To avoid the past, the present and what I thought would be my future
But then I knew, deep inside I knew
And now I know,
I know I have a problem
My name is Colleen
And I am Addict.

© Colleen Mulroney

Inside of Her

She closes her eyes
Wishing to dye
The pain is to much inside
She can't escape
There's no where to hide

Her body and soul
Are covered in scars
From a life of pain
And a razor blade

She hides herself deep inside
Where no one can reach her
So, no one can touch her
Or hurt her again

She hurts herself
To cope with it all
She doesn't like to cry
But she needs to let it out
Her mouth only Whispers
Her wounds can shout.

A Crimson Melody

Crimson tears fall down
Running away from me
Separation, dissociation
Cutting set me free

I take the blade
And slice my skin
Open wounds relief
Feeling the pain,
I'll stay sane

Emotions, memories fade
Empty inside, I want to die
Let me out of this
No more hurting
No more pain
Cutting keeps me sane

Read It, Feel It

Do you ever read a quote, and feel it in your soul?
Have you ever been so much, you feel nothing, have no tears?
Living daily with fears that are reality, and scars that people oversee, but you know
it's your souls' falling debris.
When the butterflies weigh heavy in your stomach because they are dead,
and hopes of tomorrow shed quicker than falling pet fur.
When you can't even bother in enquire about why you feel so tired,
but you know every brain required neurotransmitter will only misfire,
causing nothing short of a chaotic wildfire of thoughts,
that maybe someone should commit her, but instead and she will quickly just omit
her.

It's easier to ignore the tumbling and fumbling of emotions being over poured.
To smile when in pain, to walk contently in the rain, and numb out every single thing
that's coming from your brain.
You know most, if not all the thoughts are lies...being fed to you by depression and
suicide.
That no matter where you try to hide, or in whom you may decide to confide, the end
is near, tomorrow's have already died.

It's to Hang On

Why do I do it?
To escape the pain
The emotions and feelings
That makes me feel insane
Is there not another way?
To release the anger and the tension
I don't have one today
Cause my mind has been in confusion.
My body feels so weak
And my heart beats so fast
I barely want to speak
Why is it that I slice?
To let some of it out
It can't stay in anymore
There's no more room
For me to store
All I feel, and want to say
I tuck it away deep inside
So, no one, not even myself can find.
The truth, who I am.
Or even how I feel
What's going on?
All I hang onto
Are the two thin strings
Simple who all I've got left
Before I reach my death

My Drug

Sitting in the darkness
Pins push through my skin
The chill of fear
Spreads through my body
The fear, the panic
My head starts spinning
Racing with thoughts
Horrible memories play like a VCR
Moving ever so slowly then getting faster
Faster until I can't breathe.
Pain seeks me I need it
Like a drug, without it I suffer
It loves me and I love it
The feeling of tearing bleeding flesh
Is coolish and relaxing
Everything pauses, nothing else matters
Only the need the burning desire
For my blade, for the pain, for the blood
A painless, tearless release
The flow of crimson red tears
Through my pale thin skin
Numbness passes through my body
And through my mind
I'm emotionless, I feel nothing
Can't think, can't stop, can't die
A flick of the knife, a little pressure
The flow of blood, the heat
Escape away from reality
And the past that's not left behind

My Pain

Pitch black shadows
Dark crimson blood
Time passes unnoticed
I'm trapped inside myself
Encircled by memories
Voices and visions
The things I wish to change
But fail.

The things I hope to forget
But they are etched upon my soul
Where no one can see
And they are scared upon my flesh
So, you can see my pain.

Despair and emptiness my only company
They never seem to leave
I know them well
I've met their companions.

Suicide and hopelessness
I've sat beside them all
In my darkness, encircled by them
Kept warm by the heat
Of my blood running down my arms

© Colleen Mulroney

Night Fight

It's so much harder at night
So far, I've put up a fight
But my armour's to light
I'm torn about what's right
I'm chocking; Everything's to tight.
I'm losing my sight
I can't see the light

I'm losing this fight
The urge is too strong, My armours to light.
Cutting feels so right
No hope for the future; I lost my sight
Can't see anything at night
These walls closed in to tight

No Control

No control....
Pain filled memories
And mixed random thoughts
I'm losing control....
These feelings absorb me
Trapped inside
Longing to be free
Losing control...
I fall to the floor
Can't take anymore
Losing control...
Free my weapon
My crimson release
Losing control...
A razor sharp Exacto blade
I'm afraid,
Losing control...
Cutting my skin
Slicing deep
Losing control...
Watching veins
Searching for blood
Searching for pain
No control...

Release

Sharp silver blades
Reflect against my skin
Neatly slicing through
Blue bleeding veins
Crimson tears cry
A waterfall of pain
Flowing smoothly across my arm
They release what's within
An ugly pleasing gain
Fresh pink scars
Cover my aching body
A silent road map
Of a life painfully traveled
A memory of a true hell
Secretly unravelled

Powerful thoughts
Racing through my mind
Overwhelming me, paralysing me
Reminders of a past
Not to far behind
No escape, can't run away
Leave the body, dissociate
Brace yourself, from come what may.
Cut yourself deep and bleed
Let it out, set it free.
Life is a nightmare, a torturing dream
Breath, pain
Death, gain

Relief

Bricks are being thrown at my head
damn it I'd rather stay in bed.
Life is getting too hard
I want to be dealt a better card.

But hope is a fantasy
Not a reality
Struggling just to stay alive
Trying hard to survive

Each day that passes
Are filled with dark clouds
The visions in my head
Are getting so loud.

Depression wants to win really bad.
And all the time I feel like crying
I feel so sad
So tired all the time
Trying to fight
I want to lay down my sword
Let them kill me
And give in to the light.

Life is beating me black and blue
I don't know what to do
Trying to stay positive
Trying to believe
But I just need some relief

© Colleen Mulroney

So Far Gone

Lost in a world of pain
And crimson red tears
I'm trying to find the light again
It's been gone to many years.

But what can I do
When I hate myself and everything so much
Came so close to ending it all
Closer than ever before

Indulged in my blade
Single neat slices across my thighs
One by one they bleed
Red tears fall, a waterfall of pain.

So deep, yet not deep enough
Yet to close, past the skin to the fat
Stay away from arteries and veins or muscle
Scars so deep, they'll never heal
So much numbness can't even feel.

Lost and trapped inside my mind
Dark thoughts, black thoughts
No way out
Hope and help will I ever find
Dry your eyes no crying allowed.

Not allowed to be happy
Don't ever dare
Punish yourself
Plays through my mind
So close to death, don't even care

Will it Ever Go Away

Will the pain ever end?
The urges go away
So, I won't have to pretend
Everything's okay

Cause inside I'm screaming
My soul is bleeding and scared
I'm trying to keep on living
Why is this so hard?

Every day is a struggle.
I don't want to face
I get up each morning
Moving at a slower pace
Wanting the day to be over
So, I can cry myself back to sleep
Put my head under the pillow
And bury my face

SPOKEN WORD

Road Less Travelled

It's one minute to Midnight as I write this first line, Time passes like the wind... a gust ahead here, a gentle breeze there, or no wind at all... where the clock hand stands still, the seconds stop tic-tocking, and the silence is deafening...

I have typed out this paragraph three times, choosing different analogies only to delete them... I'm failing to find my words of expression.
I feel lost and confused and surrounded with uncertainty... I have embarked on a road less traveled where nothing is familiar, and everything unknown. It is strange and terrifying to find myself on what feels like not only a different path, but in a completely different forest.

On the journey commonly took, the trees where pillars of a diseased comfort that held out branches of false hope and leaves of opportunities that would give in to photosynthesis the moment my eyes would gaze upon them. My favorite willow trees would bow down as I would sit under them and shelter me from the creatures of the woods.

The other animals and insects that hide among the bushes were knowledgeable of my patterns of behaviour, of my fears, of my weaknesses... I was also aware of their approach tactics, and attack strategies. These woods brought about an odd ease, predictability, I know where its paths lead, it's an accustomed territory.

These new woods, and this new path is leading me on a journey I know nothing about... I am as strange to the nature along this trail, as it is to me.
It is clearly a new beginning, the roads less travelled remain that way simply because they do not provide comfort, there is reassurance when you know where you're headed.
For me these woods represent taking care of others and taking care of myself... They also represent the things I want and the things I need.

Recently I managed to distinguish between the things I have wanted along with the roads I commonly take to try to get there...VS... The things I need along with what that journey looks like. I feel as though my reality check fell from the sky and knocked me on the head... I have wanted to race forward, forget about the past, my feelings, my emotions, therapy, and follow through with my intense desire to be a functional person, caretaker, community changing volunteer and employee extraordinaire. Yet I repeated stumble... repeated burn the candle at both ends despite being aware that a candle only has so much wax to burn.

I realized that I am stumbling over the cracks and holes in my foundation, the dents and broken pieces of my sidewalks, and the confusion of who am I...

In order to progress ahead, and travel smoothly, I need to explore within to find all the broken or damaged pieces, I need to learn how to use all the tools I can find, within or taught... to repair, rebuild or even design from scratch those pieces...

Then once all the pieces are in front of me... can I begin to put the puzzle together... to discover all of who I am, and all of what I want in my life.

Depression Lies

I have learned that depression has many different faces…
Depending on the pace or days races…endurance, perseverance…
Depression is the tears behind the smile.
The upwards wrinkle in the lips that only lasts while others are looking.
That causes the bile in your stomach to do summersaults and spiral.
To feel like you're trying to defend your life, like it's on trial.
But the defence is hostile, and meanwhile your lifestyle seems only to stockpile the reasons living is not worthwhile and maybe once in awhile you'll try to not feel suicidal but still feel like the trash pile on the side of the road.
Depression is the silent screams when not saying a word but slightly thinking you'll be heard. When the tongue says I'm fine but is twisted in the form of a noose. Where you're hanging on to an absurd blurred perception that life is to be deferred, or transferred, or in need of a complex password.

When the lies of I'm okay, I'm surviving, tomorrow will be better, are more similar to an unwritten letter.
Where the silence becomes moments of emptiness, where your chest can't breathe because of its heaviness.
When the darkness becomes the pigment, your eyes are used to, and the cold dew is nothing new. When you have no clue why your brain feels like simple grey matter and misguided unconnected tissue.
Where in flickers of moments, out of the blue there's a burst of energy, and you feel like you can run free like a caribou or fly like a cockatoo but then it hits you, your skin becomes nervous tissue, residue of who and what are you, questions of what to do, what's tried and true.

Where the future seems like a preview of your past because your point of view is running through you like the stomach flu. When life feels like déjà vu, a misconstrue, a repetitive hole you just fall in to. You feel there's no way to pass through, or undo, pursue, or discover a breakthrough. Where it all feels too taboo in the worldview so silently you say adieu and the clouds and fog stick to you like super glue.
It's in times like these you realise that depression can smile… depression can laugh and have fun for awhile…

© Colleen Mulroney

Depression is deceiving, makes you feel like everyone around you is leaving, that you are the only one grieving for a life you can't find because it's weaving in and out of the light, but deep down your still believing and conceiving that somehow, someway it's worth the fight.

I Stopped Writing

I stopped writing…I had stopped. Today I sit here typing…shaking at the fear of the words that my fingers may type, nervous about the reality of the truths my mind will express, fearful of the emotions and thoughts that will seep through my fingers as they press on this keyboard; because once written in black and white…they are no longer things I can pretend don't exist, they are not hidden deep inside my barriers, they are no longer protected from being heard or felt by others…they are exposed.

Here's to brutal honesty…

I have lived my life sacrificing myself for others, it's what I know.
I know how to protect everyone else at a personal cost.
No matter the price, or the fee, no matter how lost I risk becoming,
The protected will only see the price if I let it show, let it be known; but I try so hard to keep it closed in a box, sealed tight with a black bow.
I am the strong girl, the one who is always okay, who needs to always be okay, the one who prefers to help others, who wants and needs to help others, to keep her focus there…it's easier.

I am also the broken girl, in so many pieces and shards of glass that I can't pick them up without hurting myself more.
Therefore, because I am the protector of others, and I am the strong one, and the broken one, that later fact remains as hidden as possible, for as long as possible, no matter the fee. If I can't pick up my own pieces, if I'm scared to even look at them shattered on the floor, I can not ask anyone else to do what I'm afraid to do.
Do you want to know, really know what I think of myself? Are you sure…?

I am a body and soul who is unwanted, who should not be here, a mistake…a child aborted, yet came in second… I am her disturbance, and a burden, a disgrace, not good enough, not worth anything, a plague, a child who won't disappear or die.

Her vocabulary of toxic words poisoned my own core beliefs, I believe everything she's ever said, I still react to her behaviours and actions, I don't need her to say them out loud to me although she doesn't need to because my own thoughts, my own broken brain have them on loud repeat. Her silence, lack of care, concern, and even the things unsaid remind me… And it never seems to matter how much is placed by others in my life on the other side of the scale… her words have always weighed more.

I despise myself, I can't look in the mirror, I feel that no matter how far I come, no matter the obstacles I may overcome, no matter the challenges I may conquer, deep in my core I believe I will ultimately become a statistic. Even on the good days, in the positive moments, if I search deep down trying to find that sense of hope, I continue to find that reminder, that gut feeling that no matter what, I'll become just another statistic, another could have been, another what could have been different or said, another sad story of a life unlived.

I have never liked myself, not my mind, not my body... I have tried to take in the cherished appreciation of others, their gratitude, their love...to see myself through their eyes, and I try, I really do try...and sometimes for a flicker of a moment I can see it, I can see me how they see me, but it's always just a flicker, a millisecond, and then I question...I doubt...and the tape of toxic vocabulary plays on repeat and poisons my blood, flowing through every organ, every broken piece of me.

Complicated Relationships

Overwhelming sadness, hidden anger
Feelings I am not allowed to feel.
But yet they are not buried as deep as I would like to believe.
They are rumbling to the surface, erupting like a volcano.
Covering me in their lava of guilt and shame

Why do I run from the emotions and thoughts that I need to let myself feel?
Why do I hide under my sheltered rock, in the darkness of denial?
Would the consequences be so damaging?
More than I already destroy myself.

Self sabotage and I know each other well.
We can both describe the other in perfect harmony,
Isn't that ironic...
I'm so deathly disturbed by the thoughts of letting go,
That I seem to hold on tighter to the sharp edge of the blade
Even though it hurts me, makes me bleed, I told tighter.

It seems that no matter how much it destroys me, shreds me in too little pieces.
I can't let go; I won't let go...there's a thought. I won't...
But why, what am I so afraid of...
Am I afraid that my life would get worse...no,
Remember, I know more than I reveal, think more than I say...
Therefore, I do know that life would be glorious, if only I could let go.

Afraid of happiness, scared of joy, and freedom...perhaps.
Afraid of letting go of hope, yes; nervous to let go of the very thing that keeps me going.
Hope

Hope that these storms will calm,
That the poisons I surround myself with won't kill me in the end,
That the toxic winds that knock me down will somehow let up...
Hope...I grasp to it as if my life depended on it.

© Colleen Mulroney

But hope in these things, are exactly what's killing me...
Yet self sabotage, fear, and hope are tightly holding back.
Just as much as I won't let go, they told on tightly for their dear life as well.

Will this vicious and deadly relationship end...is there hope?

Overwhelmed with Emotions

Overwhelmed with emotion, my mind is full of commotion, thoughts spinning around and around, yet verbally or out loud I don't make a sound. Putting on masks to hide the sadness every day, pretending that I'm okay. Exhaustion is my closest friend, I've come to know him well, we've intertwined so tightly I can't tell who I am without saying I'm him.

Emotions of despair, anger, and turmoil haunt my body and mind. The thought of "Why did I make that promise to Nanny?" and "When will it be okay to quit?", Yes clearly, I'm talking about suicide – that's where my thoughts go...they travel deep in to dark corners, lighting up old feelings with a flashlight saying, "Do you remember these?", I don't always yet mostly the emotions are familiar. Or they, the thoughts travel to more subtle corners of my mind, the places I keep hope or bright...and then the thoughts simply turn off the light. And it goes dark again.

I'm trying to keep fighting, trying to keep going...trying to just try, when my feelings and emotions are just saying to die. I sit in front of my computer, sending messages to friends...in them I pretend I am okay, I tell them what they want to hear me say. They want to hear that I'm getting better, that I'm in a place of moving on, moving forward, progression, not regression. I tell them that I am taking life moment by moment, and that each one is getting better, that my story is not over, that I'll get through this chapter to see the next...but they don't see my tears flowing behind the screen, they don't see the missing light in my eyes, or the wounds I constantly pick and make bleed. They don't see the need, the need to shut down because I can't cope, so it's sleep or death. Sleep that is filled with tossing and turning, waking up soaked in sweat and panic.

Death seems so peaceful, so calm and quiet...but because it is the final closing of my eyes, I choose sleep despite the fact that it does not bring peace.

I have not made up my mind yet about death...instead I still find myself weighing out the pros and cons, is there any hope, is there a change of possibly moving on, living a life different from the past. A past that I don't remember all, but know, just know so many more traumatic things happened that my mind won't allow me to be aware of, because I would break, don't open the floodgates, I will drown, I will sink, so for my sake, just pieces, feelings, emotions, flashes of memories that I don't feel are mine, dreams where I am not me, and dreams where it feels so real I wonder if it happened because every inch of my being once I wake says it did, but no conscious memory of my own do I hold, so I let it go. It's too bad I can't just let it all go, let life go, let all of me go.

© Colleen Mulroney

I can't tell if it is too early to give up, my body says I'm 32...that's at least 25 years of pain, hurt, abandonment and no self worth. Most of my life I don't remember, but the things I do remember are not happy, they are not cherished memories in which I smile, or feel good. The only person that made me feel good or that I mattered was Nanny; and now she has passed on to the heavens, where the other family members I cherished are...they say all the good die young.

Yes, Nanny was 100 years old, I believe she hung on for me...to be with me for as long as she could, my protector, my guardian. I will always be grateful for that. However now that she's gone, there's no one on my side, no one to comfort me, I am alone surround by a crowd of toxic family members, and people who say I was a mistake, that I should be locked up, and the key thrown away, crazy...delusional...a liar...that's who they say I am, because saying anything else would mean that they are not good people....... but it doesn't matter really; or maybe it does...

Sometimes I believe that this life is a punishment, that this earth is a living Hell...meant for torture and hurt. I wonder if this is all my life is meant to be...since that is all I have known. Traces of hope and glimmers of light, but ultimately darkness prevails, and wounded I lie on the ground, bleeding, sobbing, being kicked in the heart and abused. My soul is flickering...undecisive, undecided, how long do I stay.

But on the outside, in front of others...I smile, I laugh, I say positive things...and express hope. Inside I'm grieving, not only the loss of deadly people who were supposed to care for me unconditionally, but I am grieving my own life...grieving the life I wish I had, grieving the life I will most likely never have, because more often than not I know I won't make it. More often than not I know eventually I will become another statistic of failure to live to thrive, to breathe. A tragic misrepresentation of a person who thought they could overcome the challenges and obstacles that life put in the way. But I keep falling over the debris obstructing my path, and tripping over my own feet because the baggage on my shoulders weighs to heavily on my legs. I just know...the gut feeling so poignant it's unavoidable, undeniable...and most likely accurate.

I'm trying to end this vent on a positive word, but if you've listened, and really heard, really understood... there is no optimism on which to end my story, it is and will be just the end.

Perhaps I Am a Butterfly

Perhaps I am a butterfly, who can't see the colours of her wings like everyone else. The only thing I am aware and certain of it that my wings are broken, I can not fly, I am lying here on the ground, every so slowly fading away. Perhaps in the afterlife, I will soar, I will shine bright, and be able to see in a mirror the beauty of my wings...but until then, the concrete is wet and cold in this storm.

I am a sailboat, lost in the storm, with each thunder slamming down upon the waters, the boat wants to topple over, my white sails are not as white, they are hidden by a fog of darkness, the wind blows through the gaps in the threading, I am unable to adjust my sails to weather the intense waves, lightening clashes in the deep dark waters surrounding me, there's no where to go, I'm in the middle of the ocean on a broken sail boat. I am lost at sea.

I am a blue rose that grew through the grains of sand in a dessert. But a flower can not grow, blossom, or survive without water to drink, I am dehydrated and fragile, petals are falling off, piece by piece, not fixable. A flower can not regrow its petal, once gone it is forever lost, as is piece falls off, the rose falls apart and begins to die. Withering away in the dry heat, lost in the middle of the desert with no civilization in sight to rescue the flower. It can't extend its roots in hot dry sand...it has no foundation, no where to grow, or breathe. It will die, not because someone picked it from the ground, but because it was forgotten.

I am a child. An abandoned infant, longing for love of people who have decided that the child is worthless, a burden, a genetic deformity, a mistake. The child longs for affection, care, and a gentle caress from those who are supposed to help it survive, and give the child the knowledge, core beliefs, and form its basic instincts. The mind of the child is fragmented, but will not be mended, it takes others support to help a child learn, experience and grow; but this baby, this innocent life has been abandoned, forgotten and neglected. This child can not live on its own, it will be a victim of circumstance.

Everyone expresses how much of an inspiration I am to them, people express how I always get back up, mend myself, put on a bandage, and rise from the ashes like a phoenix. It doesn't feel like this time I can not heal the wounds, or put both feet on the ground, my solid foundation has crumbled into pieces, where do I stand, how to I rise again without the pile of ashes that the dark winds have blown away. Pieces of me gone, scattered in the air, I am unable to collect them, they are ashes...the have dispersed into thin air, never to be seen again.

How many times does it take when one falls down a pitch black well of depression, but one decides that enough is enough, and refuses to try that one more time. When am I allowed to say, I'm done! The candle has burned through both ends, the wax is spread out and melted, the string of strength holding the candle together has burnt through and exists no more. Hope has faded to darkness and the light is buried under a thick dark fog that nightmares are made of. There's no help, you can't repair a butterfly's wings with words, or will it to heal back together so it can fly away. It has one fate, and that fate will eventually set it free. I am the string in the candle, I am the child, I am the blue rose, I am the sailboat, and I am the broken winged butterfly.

Not Good Enough

Not good enough, you're not good enough…. echoes inside my head… I'm not good enough, great now I say it to myself I realize…
I cut myself down with the toxic words of others that were carved into my core and my whole being. I destroy myself from the inside like they used to hit me on the outside and the loud repetitive toxic vocabulary they used it shouted at me by my own unmoving mouth.

I will never be good enough…a daily thought that leads to people pleasing and burn out; because I'm constantly trying too hard to give my whole being to every single individual that is around me. But I am only one being…not 2, not 5, not 10. And even though burn out is the consequence … self destruction is the meaning between the lines. Remember they said, you're not good enough. I remember that I'm never going to be good enough.

I see myself from the outside, running and on the go like I have an internal battery or one on my back – like the Energizer bunny, I keep going and going and going…until the battery is low, but then I keep going and going…and going, until the battery died, I am my own worst foe.

The negative part of self awareness is that I can clearly see the self sabotage in me, I abuse my self like they taught me. They, those people are not involved in my everyday life anymore but it's like I picked up where they left off, and even though they walked out, or I shut the door, I keep knocking myself to the floor.

And when I am on the floor, knocked down, sometimes I stay there for awhile…looking at the cracks in the ground and comparing them to the cracks in my skin, I look at the dirt and grim around me and compare it to the dents and bruises within. I ponder now if I should stand up if I should follow that quote, "Fall seven, stand up Eight". But deep down there is so much hate. A disgust pointed in the wrong direction, when the storm hits a boat adjusts it's sails, but the sails got thrown backwards and the waves sent the boat down the river in the wrong direction…but wait…what if the boat tips over, what if the storm doesn't let up, what if…what if…what if the constant worry and questions of what ifs are like a hurricane out of nowhere that the boat isn't prepared for…but down the river if flows…in the wrong direction.
Do I stand up…Do I take down the sails, take out my ore and paddle against the current. Do I try once more? …

Of course, I try once more...the crowd on the shore is cheering paddle harder with that single ore, you can do it, we believe in you, fight...get up...try another door. And the people pleaser get's up off the floor, dusts herself off...and tries once more.
All while hearing loud and clear the crowd on the shore applauding her efforts...she also hears the crowd gathered up on the bridge screaming we don't want you anymore.
And with both groups cheering and screaming she fights within herself, torn between keeping going and going...and slamming closed the door. The constant battle between good and evil, between those who society says are supposed to love you, and those who just do, between living for others and living for herself...
She is me...I battle daily, fighting against the ingrained automatic thoughts of not good enough for those that are supposed to... vs ... the good enough for those that just do.

My war cry is silent...my screams come out as whispers, and I don't know how to reach out. Because my first response is, I'm alone, there's no one there to help...I was a child often left to fend for myself and I often had too, so I did. So, to reach out for support is so incredibly foreign, strange, and unreal...to believe that there is someone on the other side of the door when I'm needing help and want to reach out, is so seemingly unbelievable that I fall to the floor.

And once again I compare the cracks in the ground to the cracks in my skin...I compare the gaping holes in the floor to the deep wounds in my soul, and I take a moment to breathe...in...out...in...out...in...out...And I the people pleaser and the battle warrior, the one lost on the boat arriving at the shore finally make a decision to ignore the screaming on the bridge...I can't deal with that anymore, and as for the wounds in my soul and the cracks in my skin...well don't they say: when there's a piece of glass missing in a tinted broken window that still stands strong, isn't that how the light gets in?

Pause

Pause, let your mind focus on what it takes to live... focus on a complete respiratory cycle, breathe in ...and breathe out. Pause... Put your hand over your heart... thump thump... thump thump... the beating of your heart pumping blood throughout your body...

You are living... right now in this moment you are alive. Your body is doing all the necessary procedures to allow you to live. But my question is, you're alive... but are you living? Do you thrive each moment that you are alive, do you strive to reach your goals to allow your dreams to come true... do you have a dream? Do you have a passion? Do you allow yourself to have compassion for the hopes of tomorrows that can become todays, these right now moments...?

The future by definition is: 1. A noun, meaning: the time or a period of time following the moment of speaking or writing; time regarded as still to come.

So, in the time to come... each moment is a choice, a decision, to be alive... or to live...
to follow old patterns of routine and behaviour or to create new ways to spend and behave in this ... in your lifetime. It's not a crime, it's a possibility of a full time... internal rhyme of something anything different between your moment of the routine caffeine, hygiene, and cuisine...work my body like it's a machine... How do you feel? Are you locked in a life of need, ignoring your wants? What about your desires, dreams, passions... are they outside the box thinking that doesn't fit in with your conditioned response...? What if you allowed yourself to create your own renaissance? To start a new from this moment on... to step outside the box, take a key and open all the locks that incarcerate your future like a vending machine. You don't need the proper change or dollar bills to buy a better tomorrow... you just need to intervene and believe in the unseen.

The future by definition is: 2. An adjective, meaning at a later time; going or likely to happen or exist.

Going to happen, likely to happen, to exist... the possibilities of change and choice are endless. The next moment is yet to come... you are still alive... take these next few minutes to think about the rest of the time that you are alive. What does it look like... how does it feel...?

Are you marking off the items on your to do list or check list... what is you dismiss your waiting list and give your life a twist...and in the midst of change allow your self to persist and insist that your passions and dreams on not on the blacklist?

Hope... tomorrow can be about what you want, steps can be taken to follow your dreams and passions. You are limitless...
The strongest, most dedicated people are those who persevere through hardships. The most able people are those who regardless of life experiences stay aboard the ship. It's crystal clear, that if you adhere despite the fear, you volunteer to become your own engineer and design your life to not just be alive, but to live.
So that next time someone tells you to pause... complete a respiratory cycle... and feel your heart beating... and asks if you are alive to survive... or living ... you can answer that you're beginning, existing, and greeting with open arms a vital arrival of revival and living each moment, each second, minute, hour, and day... not just living, or breathing for survival, but giving your self compassion to allow yourself to be living your passion.

What's Left?

How do I go on living every day?
Fighting for each moment searching for words to say
Why do I open my eyes if only to see darkness painful tears with goodbyes?
Why is my world so crazy with mixed emotions?
Making my vision so unclear and hazy
Does everything need to be hard so many lessons to learn?
And the good moments you have to earn.
Just to read and enjoy Empty words written on a card.
Yesterday was painful, today not worth seeing.
So why should there be a tomorrow Why continue being.
If only to continue this fighting and climbing this steep hill
Getting no closer to the top because I mess up and take a spill.
Hope has faded and faith left my sight.
All that's left is the mysterious dark night.
When dreams have perished, and the ropes untied
There's nothing left holding me from jumping off the cliff I'm on
Is there a reason for me to be like another person?
I make plans for tomorrow not to let others worry or to drag them into my sorrow.
Keep them happy let them see plans one less worry they hold in their hands.
Backing away from them all will make it less painful for them can't you see.
So, if the time comes and I take my hard fall, less hurt for them they won't remember
me.
And I you see can finally be carefree.
Cause when I look back at my life and all I've been through.
I can't even get to or through all these walls I've put up.
I can't erase my nightmares of the past,
They flow through like a train ride, each passing by so fast yet leaving enough
moments.
To focus on each one, it's there how these feelings last.
They never go away and seem impossible to forget.
Do you think you can help I doubt it, you want to bet you have no idea?
No one can help, yet they all seem to try.
They say they understand, can't they tell I know the lie.

© Colleen Mulroney

To go through all I have and still take a breath today.
I admit is some accomplishment, yet many think I'm strong, but I know I'm weak.
I'm the one who goes crazy and runs to the street.
I'm the one who dreams of dying, letting all things go.
But I say I'm weak cause its to hard to do.
I want everything to be easy and simple just for once.
They say the good get all the shit, but they also say the good dye young.
I say maybe its true that the good are unlucky.
But I'm supposed to be the good, then how come I'm still alive.
Cause if I were dead, it'd be way to easy the world doesn't seem to be through with me.
I've tried and tried to die yet nothing works, lets me succeed.

Refocus

At times, it gets hard to see in the dark. I feel like I'm traveling through a never-ending tunnel of unanswered questions, uncertainty, and overwhelming emotions stamped with an exclamation mark!
Spiraling down fast, the outside closing in like a funnel, I want to see the light; but this darkness is stuck to me, like it was born on me like a birthmark.
I need to force myself to find some positivity, build up my creativity, discovery some uplifting extracurricular activities, and allow myself to accept my sensitivity.
Gratitude feels like a good place to start, to stop myself from falling apart, jumpstart my focus into creating a work of art, let show my bleeding heart, and to take part in an auto-restart.
Easier said than done to look on the bright side, to change my perspective on things that I have misidentified, unqualified because my mind has been preoccupied.
My Jekyll and Hyde way of thinking leaves me dissatisfied, petrified, and trying to heal my soul with peroxide. I need to make a list to untwist my scared wrist and continue to persist.
On this day, the world is full of technology to appreciate, an everlasting supply of means to communicate any emotional state.
There's a multitude of ways to reinvigorate, rejuvenate, and recreate my dull blank slate into everything that will stimulate me to fill my plate, with the extraordinarily little things to the tremendous, that I can appreciate, and let it motivate me to celebrate all the things I've taken for granted.
It's time to dedicate today, this date, this moment, to state that life is not black and white, to shine a light on the simplest delight, to recentre my line of sight, because moment by moment eventually everything will be alright, and during the harder times where I feel like I'm losing the fight…I only need take out my pen and write.

A road to recovery
A possible journey

This poem is for the lost and found, who've been tossed around, who've been crossed by their loved ones, who decided to get up and stand their ground, who have chosen to make their heart the strongest muscle they've got, who want to begin anew, with a clean slate.

- It's going to be lit tonight, all my friends will be there!
- It's 5 O'clock somewhere, so who cares!
- I finally fit in! I feel free to be me!
- The pain is gone; I found a relief!

- It's my freewill, my responsibility, I don't care about genetic history!
- I'm ok, I'm fine! Stop judging me so quickly!
- I need to escape this hell-bent life, leave me alone to forget my pain and strife!
- It's better than the alternative, yeah yeah I know to a certain degree, besides it's not that bad, it's not a catastrophe!

When I was young I only knew how to survive, I didn't have the sophistication to cope with life's trials, twists and turns, so instead I looked for every which way to escape, orbit out of my mind, float space bound in numbness, detached and depersonalised.
Maybe for you it was that tingle down your spine, the knowing sensation in the back of your mind, the instant feel better... following the leader, or trying to be a trend setter. Playing pretend with a desire of just wanting to fit in. It became the easiest way, it worked so perfectly, that anxiety vanished, and the depression and loneliness perished.
Or maybe you wanted an exit from the reality you were currently in, a form of escape from the crap you've been through... wanting to calm yourself, protect yourself, embalm yourself, hide yourself from the pain... a release from your problems, from the things you couldn't handle, paralysing the emotions that were too overwhelming to deal with... to stop your thoughts from spinning, close the door behind where all the chaos and commotion remain hidden, maybe it was your personal locksmith.
Or perhaps it was a mix of all or little of the previously mentioned that was enough to entice, and in desperation, wanting relief, we turned to what cost us the highest price... simply because it's what felt nice.

This was our demise, telling ourselves it wouldn't hurt to try, to step away from all the dull colours caging us in, believing what would eventually be our own lies. We tried to keep living life blinded to the reality that the objective evidence would suggest... because everything feels alright, and no one really knows what we did last night, we didn't know we had become obsessed, and for many loved ones in our lives they may never have guessed, the amount of fear or pain we compressed in order to suppress the distress, and torturing unrest that heated the fires deep within our core... keeping everything unaddressed, leaving us feeling depressed, more distressed, until eventually we realised that in order to make progress, we needed to request somewhere to confess, decompress, express, and assess just how much we had regressed, and reinvest in ourselves, to let our voices be heard, open up the locked doors, and get all the torment off our chest.

Our future wasn't bright, and we were stuck in this tunnel where at the end, we couldn't see the light. We walked around with a damaged view of the concept of any hope or any self respect which were the two things we've managed to lose... so confused, and now at a fork in the road, with an option to choose... and we had heard all the why's, the moments of feeling to low to try, to lost to cut off all the ties, but we didn't want to die...

We had asked substance to take the pain away, but we didn't invite it to take the joy with it too. It made us feels numb, we knew what it was doing all along and we liked that... so we questioned why fight that.

But standing in our shoes and coming to this place... we got slapped in the face with bittersweet taste that people stilled cared and welcomed us with a warm embrace. And even though the hope in ourselves had faded, and we felt completely alienated, we knew we were stuck, struggling, stumbling, digging out our own graves which we could of easily slip into, we wanted to find a reason to live... when we thought asking for help would be the hardest step to take, when we thought we had nothing left to lose.

But still for some afraid of the commitment, paralysed, afraid, lost in a state of denial, believing their habit is under control, they refuse to let go, swearing they are strong enough to make it, but we know realistically, addiction is a disease, there's no six degrees of separation between us and them...the chemicals alter our brains, it's chemistry.

What you've done in your past doesn't have to define you. Addiction doesn't discriminate, it doesn't care if you're a millionaire or on welfare; so, there's no need to compare. If you have the urge to repair, hang on to it, don't let go.

© Colleen Mulroney

Our souls long to recover, we want to be freed, we long to be whole, we are the ones who have asked for helped, and received... Beaver opened the door, for us to come through, to remember our dreams, to believe in our goals, to rediscover who we really are, and our souls. Replacing our feelings of emptiness and dangerous sinkholes, starting with letting go of control, with hard work and digging deep inside, and filling out the homework in the binders in our cubbyholes. We let down our walls brick by brick and talked about our issues, while the people around us handed us tissues. We reached out and grabbed the hand offering us another chance. We looked our addiction straight in the eyes, determined to fight, and here finally our futures are starting to look bright.

We have the courage to learn the tools and the knowledge on how to use them. We've all here together, we're facing the storm, bad weather isn't forever, we're breaking the norm.
From there we have the opportunity to dive into amazement, to see the possibility of happiness, discover that sense of belonging, being, purpose, and potential. We don't want to relapse, or hit more rock bottoms, we know there is no joy in the bondage that was keeping us hostage.

Now we can see a light in the dark, and beacon in the night. We are building a foundation, a level ground to start fresh on, we are breaking free from our insecurities, surrendering to vulnerability, exposing our truths, the fears of not being strong enough, good enough, or.... Enough, are starting to disappear. And we know when the nights feel never-ending or life too hard, our 20/20 hindsight can be blinding, reminding us to hold on; that life can be mesmerizing. We have grown, we are reaching milestones, and reaching out to each other to calm the unknown. We don't have to face anything or ever be alone.

Can you see it? Can you feel it? I'm so grateful to be here. We are caterpillars emerging from our cocoons with beautiful, coloured wings, Phoenix's rising from our discouraged ashes, filling our voids by changing our perspectives, and drinking from half full or refillable glasses.

Today is all we have, today we will not use, today is our day and a good day, today we stand tall. Today we won't regret it, today we are recovering, Today is one day, One day at a time. Today we can look back and say Today I am sober; I can make it after all.

Untitled

I feel lost in a dark forest, surrounded by a never-ending turf of trees, and gloom.
I wear so many masks to hide my soul's expression, to cover my emotions I wear costumes.
I linger and crawl, using every ounce of strength to get out of bed when morning comes.
I stagger and lean against the walls to hold me up...I have lost my equilibrium.

Even with open eyes I see only shadows, fog, shades of black... there is no light.
I repeat to myself as I have for decades that tomorrow may offer me a flashlight.
To see further ahead in this never-ending tunnel of pain, sadness, and despair
That somewhere, there's a way out of this nightmare warfare, and I'll breathe actual air.

Fatigue, depression, and hopelessness are ingrained to my core, I can't take it anymore.
I am losing this battle, I'm too far from shore, I sometimes wish my life was a lie, a metaphor.
All a big evil joke, that keeps making me choke on thick smoke, hallucinating from heatstroke.
That one day I'll be able to evoke like magic, provoke my true life to stop hiding, uncloak.

The way I'm surviving day to day is not how I want to occupy one more tomorrow.
Walking on a very thin piercing edge with vertigo, stuck incommunicado, hello?
Is anyone out there...do you see my invisible wounds...hear my silenced screams?
Can you perceive the colourless bloodstreams, is this the torrent I follow...my life's theme?

I want to become so insignificant, bones... when I turn sideways, I'd disappear.
So, I can stay veiled from predators and narcissists, I can't handle the souvenirs.
Can I drink an elixir, reappear, and adhere to the world of Shakespeare?
This life is too hard to steer, too severe, bursting of fear, yet I suppress the shed of a solitary tear.

Unable to express the slightest emotion, they're imprisoned tight within my ribcage, stuck.

Even if bluntly hit by a truck, the havoc will not pour out the poison detained in my stomach.
Lost, blinded, bleeding, hopeless, despaired, pleading, hiding, feeling utterly handicapped,
There's no way out, wrapped in death, suffocating, strapped to nothingness, trapped.

I've lost the battles, I'm losing the war...my reservoir is empty, in the sky there's no guiding star.
My skin full of scars is a roadmap to my memoir.
A life predestined to be forgotten, shouldn't have existed in the first place, consequence suffering.
Now incapacitated, disoriented, depersonalized, moment by moment my life is hemorrhaging

Emotions are okay – A reminder.

Thoughts inside my head transfer to the words on this once blank page, it doesn't take long for me to type out the chaos in between, to explain what I mean.
Luckily, I can type about as fast as I can think, no editing involved, It's a direct link.
Pours out naturally from my mind to my fingers and appears on my screen. Mental hygiene, cleansing machine, a useful tool to use in this time of quarantine. Express myself, release myself, free myself from containing it all within, Poetry is healthier for my sanity than a dose of a benzodiazepine.
An emotional whirlwind that is transgressing moment to moment, is at times overwhelming, distressing, however I hold on to each second, each blessing, each chance to realise I'm not regressing, or repressing but progressing, and expressing my inner dialogue.
I'm not letting these times that can be depressing, downright stressing swallow me whole. Instead, I am accessing and addressing my inner self depreciating catalogue, changing my one direction monologue, and sorting out my hazed brain fog.
It's completely normal to be all over the map, I'm human, you're human...I'm not going to sugar coat it or cover it with bubble wrap. I'm reminding myself that emotions are not a booby trap to be avoided, they are not a mousetrap waiting to snap, or a shaken soft drink about to burst off it's bottle cap, they are not a sand trap that I want to sink in to, so talking about emotions without becoming disjointed is my top priority.
Writing is unapologetically my own personal session of psychotherapy, to vent with honesty, to regain clarity, to lessen my anxiety, continue my sobriety, and voluntarily dive in to self care, it's my warranty, that I can get through this uncertainty, and maintain a mentality of reality daily by concurrently moving finger after finger on this keyboard, letting out the vulnerability of my emotional instability, and continuing to describe what's usually lower rated in popularity...and by letting go, and freely designing word after word with each keystroke, I know I'll find some quality in these times of confusing normality.

The Day I Dreaded Most

I don't know where to begin…to express just how much you mean to me, to express just how much I love you, need you, and just how much I miss you.

On Sunday, March 26th at 12:30pm my cell phone rang…I almost didn't answer it…I was about to go into a training session…It was also my mother, your daughter…with whom I never connected with…because of my mother's toxicity I almost didn't answer…but something inside of me said I should, especially since my mother knew where I was and what I was doing.

My mother was calling…
I knew instantly something was wrong…it had to be important…but I was ready…armed with fighting words…a vocabulary of distrust, disappointment, and years of hurt.

She spoke…I held up my shield to protect myself from what my mother would usually say… But in one sentence…I fell to the floor…disarmed, scarred, broken, and crying…begging…" You're lying" …" Don't do this to me" …" Not today" ….
The mix of words combined were a compilation that formed the sentence, I never wanted to hear, that I never wanted to echo in my mind. "Nanny is dying" …three simple words…5 syllables that would change my life forever… and alter my entire world into chaos.

My Nanny…was my sun in which my world orbited around. Nanny was… the water that hydrated my dreams, hope, and strength so they could grow, flourish, and bloom. But with 12 letters of the alphabet and two spaces in between…everything stood still….and suddenly the darkest and quickest eclipse covered my sun…blinding me from it's bright, positive, and comforting rays, my apocalypse had begun.

With dread in my heart, and the most bittersweet sadness in my soul, I walked into your room. The blinds were open, and the earths sun was shinning through, covering you in beams of light, but the silence was too loud, too intense to grasp…and I ran out for a moment. Clutching my chest and holding my breath…panic, fear, grief… "I'm lucky" … I remember thinking – "I get to say goodbye" … and even though dread coursed through my veins, and images of life's beautiful, cherished moments flooded my memory; the ambivalence of denial and your freedom from Dementia and Alzheimer's tore me to shreds.

But I walked back in... I remember looking at you, sleeping on your bed...I took everything in and tried to ingrain the image of you in my head.

Your head was resting ever so gently on the pillows...your chest still breathed up and down.... I grabbed your hand; I can still feel it's warmth...I held tight. Your eyes were closed...I ached to see them one last time. But I remembered that the twinkle in your eyes had long passed...I wanted you to see me, hold me, comfort me one more time... but your memory of who I was...had long faded.

I took a few deep breaths... taking in all I could of your beauty... each wrinkle which expressed the stresses, the happiness, and the joys...a long life well lived. Your lips... used to speak gentle words of reassurance, and kindness. Your ears... used for listening so intently they ran their course much before as well. Yet, on my knees, kneeling right up beside you, as close as I could get... I knew you could hear me.

I spoke gently... with words of reassurance...just like each time you spoke to me. As tears quietly flowed down my cheeks, I gathered each piece of strength that you be stilled in me, and I told you, that you could go... that it would be okay... that I would be okay... that you could rest eternally in peace... that I would be okay... I knew, I knew with every molecule in my body, soul, and mind...that you were waiting for me to reassure you that I would be okay...

And even though most days still...I regret making you the promise that I would be okay without you...especially since every moment of life with you... I promised myself I wouldn't live without you... especially... especially since I couldn't and never wanted to even begin to imagine life without my sun.

How can a world survive in the darkness... how can flowers bloom without proper hydration, love, and tender care? How could I go on without you, my Nanny?
As I write this...50 minutes remain until it will be exactly 365 days to the moment my phone rang. I have survived almost an entire year without holding your hand, seeing your smile, hugging you and feeling your arms wrap around me.

I have survived... but I have not yet allowed myself to live...the thought of living without you is still so beyond terrifying that for now...I am only willing to survive. That thought...those words...that I just echoed... are at the same time as true, as they are an epiphany to me.

This past year...these last 12 months.... these past 365 days...these last 8,760 hours...these past 525,600 minutes I have refused to live... I have only allowed myself to survive... But I made you a promise... "That I would be okay" ... so maybe today... however maybe only tomorrow, or the next day, or month, or year... I will start to learn how to live without you, but for now... all I can do is survive...and remember you and all that includes, memories, words, encouragement, support, and a never-ending supply of hope. Until next time Nanny...I love you!

Your Granddaughter and baby girl,

I Remember

I remember, do you remember?

Watching Laurence Welk shows, and walking Lady?
Do you remember dancing with Papa at Son's of Scotland events...?
Do you remember, phone conversations that could last an hour, and getting ready
for my prom...the beautiful white pearls, I now treasure in the jewelry box that Papa
made you. ...do you remember?
Before you died, you died inside...the slow leak of memory draining from your mind
over time, lead to nothingness. A body that became an empty shell, the light in your
eyes darkened by fear, fear of the unknown, the strange people who surrounded you
– that you used to call family. Little by little our names faded away, flowing gently
through the sky, yet fast as if our identities were soaring on eagle's wings.
Today, your portrait hangs in my living room, my common space...it's one of many
pictures I have of you...pictures that trigger memories – happy, yet painful. They
hurt so much because I can't remember them with you, you're not here....and before
you left, 5 years of torture where you didn't remember....
You slide away, through my fingertips, and I couldn't hold on, you glistened through
my grasp like oil and water, I couldn't mix them...I, your granddaughter, your
cherished, ever so loved, and precious Colleen...forgotten, locked in the black
wooden box of dementia, with a lock so fierce, no hammer, no bolt cutters, no love –
could unlock it.
I miss you today, but I've been missing you for many moons, suns have risen, and
suns have set, you were so close...yet so far. I long to hear your voice, how I wish I
had saved a voicemail with a personal message from you, how I long to see your
delicate cursive composing me a letter of memory. Instead, I have pictures, hundreds
of pictures...but no voice do I hear, no laugh, no smell, no comfort.
I think of you daily – as I always have, but now I'm alone. Only each day so I long for
your presence, ... To feel you near me, to hear the words "I love you – Don't give up".
I made you a promise on your death bed, many express their point of view – at least
you got to say goodbye, but did I? could you hear me, did you know it was me.... I
should have said goodbye when you knew my name and the echo of my voice. It
happened so fast, yet so agonizingly slow...I watched the illness take pieces of
you...each day, each moment, each time I saw you, little by little, piece by piece, the
illness stole you away from me, it took you away from me before I could even
comprehend that you, my nanny, were leaving me.
I may have said goodbye, I even promised to keep on keeping on, keep living, keep
breathing, keep fighting...without you. You, nanny, you were everything....my

inspiration, the air that filled my lungs, the wind that adjusted my sails, and steered me to safety. How do the stars shine without a sky to twinkle in? how does the tree grow without a solid foundation of earth to spread its roots. Lost...I feel lost, lost and alone in a world I didn't' want to live in without you. I struggle to find the light of the stars, I ache to find the willingness to open my eyes and face each moment, tom make new memories in my life, and take pictures...pictures with a missing piece. The missing piece is you nanny. Like a puzzle that can not be finished, ...because of the absent part...part of me is missing, is dead, is wondering around like a lost animal, searching for it's home, a sense of familiarity, a feeling of belonging, and something comforting. I'll never find it, dementia took away too many pieces...it took all of you, it took you away forever; and I feel forever will I be lost.

Destruction

I'm falling apart,
I can see the darkness flowing all around me.
I have no energy, so I let them be,
knowing full well that it wants to consume me.
I have no ability to care anymore
I say I'm fine, because it's easier to say, than to try and explain why I'm not feeling
okay.

Withdrawn, quiet, lost in the gush of toxic thoughts
Waves of emotions flooding my lungs... I'm drowning.
Darkness, hopelessness, there's no air.
Silently screaming through crimson cracks,
Quickly suffocating underneath the weight of despair.
I'm not meant for this world, for this life.
I hold the control but no power over its side effects.
The hurricane of devastation that would rip through the souls I've touched.
I couldn't offer consolation towards the pain, all because I want mine to end so
much.

Every day I'm reminded of the battles I've fought
Each moment I lose more hope towards the life I sought
Spinning in chaos, a whirlwind of self destruction
Dizzy and weak, once the tornado stops, I'm on the floor
I can't continue this journey, I'm too broken and damaged in my core

I want to soar away, disappear,
This life will probably end as I fear
Trying to withdraw from everyone, even those that are dear.
If everyone saw me how I see myself, they would understand...
They'd run for the hills, hide, comprehend...

35 years old, yet my book is filled with more suffering than 10 lifetimes
No matter how tight I hold the pen to write my own story
There no promissory note that I'll be freed from this purgatory,
Instead the only constants are gory ambulatory chapters,
Nighttime's filled searching for past times, and rhymes.

© Colleen Mulroney

Unable to conceive a new version of me, a being free
Reality is people are hurt by my falling debris,
and there's no guarantee, only my plea, to accept my apology
and even with technology,
there's no escaping my pathology, biology, neurology, or psychology...

Ode to Me

This is an ode to myself, my lost forgotten soul.
I know you're somewhere inside of me, misplaced,
waiting to be set free, hoping I uncover the healing skeleton key.
I'm desperate to find you, get this life under some stable form of control,
be able to crawl out of this deep rabbit hole,
black hole of depression and despair.
I want to feel whole, I want to care, breath pure fresh air,
and dare to live and not survive.
Find a purpose, a reason to be, that makes me happy, a goal.
I want to thrive, doing something with my life that makes me crave and want to be
alive.
No more feeling like trash, this body doesn't want to crash, or turn in to an urn of
just ash.
Deep down there must be a stash of energy, of positivity, a will to be, an urge to
discover my potential.
Certainly, there is more to me.
Dreams and desires, Hopes and a purpose,
something that will light the fires of motivation,
that will rearrange my brains wires to obtain a healthy level of determination.
I long to acquire whatever I'm missing.
and require to get out of this lost low drowning sea of stagnation, no more
procrastination. It's time for whatever it takes, what ever habits I need to break or
create.
It feels like it's now or never, to give it all I've got,
get the recommended support I've sought.
Brave through the unknown, meet and follow my true destiny, fate, opt out of this
hell bound loop of eight, and move forward, rise above, set myself free...Be ME!

ABOUT THE AUTHOR

Colleen Mulroney

Born and raised in Montreal, Quebec. Colleen is a bilingual young woman who discovered her love for writing poetry in her early teenage years. Her high school English teachers helped nourish her writing abilities. Friends, family and professionals continued to encourage Colleen to keep using poetry as a healthy way of self expression. Used to triumph over destructive thoughts and help fight against depression and other dark or intrusive thoughts.
Colleen continues to be an active advocate for Mental Health, promoting awareness and helping battle stigma. She strongly believes in openly talking about Mental Health and hopes that one day it will be discussed the same as any health condition.